The Juno Charm

Nuala Ní Chonchúir

salmonpoetry

Published in 2011 by
Salmon Poetry
Cliffs of Moher, County Clare, Ireland
Website: www.salmonpoetry.com
Email: info@salmonpoetry.com

ISBN 978-1-907056-64-2

COVER IMAGE: *Midnight Peacock by Anni Betts – www.annibetts.com*
COVER DESIGN: *Siobhán Hutson*

PRINTED IN IRELAND BY GEMINI

*Salmon Poetry receives financial support from
The Arts Council / An Chomhairle Ealaíon*

for my darling daughter, Juno

Acknowledgements

Thanks go to the editors of the following publications, in which some of these poems first appeared:

Abridged; *Art Now Art Book*; *Avalon*; *Buzz* – a Templar Poetry anthology; *Best of Irish Poetry 2010* anthology; *Crannóg*; *Galway – City of Strangers* anthology; *Heroe's Congress – Dublin Poetry Review*; *Indieoma*; *Ink, Sweat & Tears*; *Ink, Sweat and Years* – a 2008 anthology from *Ink, Sweat and Tears*; *Junction 14.5*; *La Paume Ouverte* – Festschrift for Francoise Connolly; *Loqacious Placemat*; Mannequin Envy; *Mapping Me* anthology; *Marks* – a Circa / Stinging Fly publication; *Melusine*; *Other Poetry*; *Photograph Prose*; *Poetry Ireland Review*; Popshot; *Portrait of the Artist with a Red Car* (a Templar Poetry pamphlet), *Postcard Poems*; *Revival*; *Ropes 2011*; *Southword*; *Strand* anthology; *Swansea Review*; *The Chimaera*; *The Gulper Eel*; *The Poetry Bus*; *The SHOp*; *The Stinging Fly*; *The Stony Thursday Book* 2008; *The Stony Thursday Book* 2009; *The Watchful Heart – A New Generation of Irish Poets: Poems and Essays* – a Salmon anthology.

An illustrated version of the poem 'Dancing with Paul Durcan' appeared in the No Grants Gallery Writing Exhibition, Temple Bar, Dublin, May 2009.

An illustrated version of the poem 'The Juno Charm' appeared in the exhibition 'Hunt the Postcard', The Hunt Museum, Limerick, November 2009.

'Frida Kahlo Visits Ballinasloe' was placed second in the inaugural Black Diamond Poetry Competition in 2010.

'On Being Irish' (titled 'Freedom') appeared as a poster in Dublin, as part of UpStart's arts campaign. UpStart is a non-profit arts collective which put creativity at the centre of public consciousness during the Irish General Election Campaign in February 2011.

Thanks to Salmon Poetry, especially Jessie and Siobhán. To my family, especially Ma, Da, Úna, Finbar, Cúán, Finn, Juno and John. To my friends Órfhlaith, Karen and Marcella for literary chats, support and fun. To the members of the Group 8 Artist's Collective and also my writing group, The Peers, especially Patrick Chapman. Special thanks to Mary O'Donnell, an inspirational writer and woman.

Thanks to the Tyrone Guthrie Centre at Annaghmakerrig where some of these poems were written.

Thanks to artist Anni Betts whose beautiful 'Midnight Peacock' makes a perfect cover image.

CONTENTS

Aubade for Extraordinary Life

In the afterglow, I watch your bear-like doze,
snout tucked under one tattooed arm.

The dawn starts its chorus, needing a witness, so
I part the curtains and see a crow toss its wings

into a hero's cloak before skydiving from phone-wires;
a cloud hangs like a balloon on a contrail string.

You father and mother me, sister and brother me,
though our heat and fervour don't talk of that,

no, it's not our nights that say all about us,
but our days and our nights, the hours dwindled

in the ordinary sharing and partings of life:
a dinner made together, lunches packed in schoolbags,

bedtime stories read, the call of each Monday morning
that sees you bound for the train, me to my desk.

All around it hovers our love, rich and sure as honey
lifted from the bee-furred heart of a sunflower.

Under This Painting, We Sleep

In the painting over our bed,
the Flatiron is purple and phallic.
It stands, steadfast,
not moving. It is you.

And I am the pink skyscraper
that looms in the corner of the canvas,
domineering and watchful,
wanting to be all of Manhattan.

We are reaching, both of us,
into a yolk-yellow sky,
reaching for the plate of the moon
that is slung over Madison Square.

And the clouds are like Irish clouds,
so near to the city they are part of it;
they creep across our rooftops,
skimming water-towers like a blessing.

Below us, in our bed, we sleep.

Valentine's Day

In our hotel on Lexington Avenue
our bodies call to each other across the bed;
the Chrysler Building dips to our window,
lit up like a satisfied voyeur;
while sirens serenade from the East River
answering the songs on the streets:
fire trucks, patrol cars, trash cans,
the catcalls of pros and pimps.
Air gushes up from subway grates,
wraps comfort around the needy.
Below us, the ghosts of Turtle Bay cattle
shuffle in their slaughterhouse pens.
We steal heat through our skins,
safe from the wind that hurtles up the island.

Chinatown, New York

On Canal Street hawkers
offer fake Rolex and Prada
in broken English whispers,
but through the heart of the town
shab and colour collide
where the shops spill
wares onto street stalls:
pots of osmanthus jelly,
tang's salted eggs,
wife cakes, husband cakes,
joss sticks, dried lilies,
Healthy Boy soy sauce,
yellow-tinned fried dace,
a triad of tapioca pearls,
Heaven and Hell bank notes,
plate-sized discs of rice paper,
sweet olives in plastic bags,
pale as boiled gooseberries.
All I buy is a jade Buddha.
I rub his potbelly for luck.

Airwaves

You say I am more
canal than river.

Today, unlike myself, I concur.
Even I can be agreeable
on the right occasion.

And what an occasion:
I have old – wampum beads,
a silver peacock – new,
borrowed – wrist-slung pearls,
Airwaves, unchewed – blue.

On Avenue of the Strongest
we swap rings.
On Avenue of the Americas
we eat our fill.
We stroll Fifth to Madison Square.

Here we sit in our
newly minted marriage
in the evening heat.

Today I am more
river than canal.

This Is No Cana

after Stanley Spencer

The wedding breakfast is eaten
and our guests are idling;
there is no handy miracle man
to turn good water to better wine.

My bride is regretful
about the poverty of our feast.

'What can we do?' I say to her,
my mind on our honeymoon –
the raw velvet of her opening,
the soft suck of skin over skin.

'Let them eat cake,' she says,
and I'm glad that I've married her.

Straw Widow

Monday is putting in time,
Tuesday, the longest day,
Wednesday, a frisson –
a swell between my legs
while I track your journey
from industrial estate,
to train, to bigger train;
the final stretch is your walk
from the station to home,
and me: your straw widow.

Fairy Light Lingerie

after Soozi Roberts' video art

I wish I had some fairy light lingerie:
a red bulb-rope to wrap around me
in our darkened room.

I would lie there – a radiating x-ray
over the covers – each flash revealing
a breast, a thigh, a V of hair.

I would wait like a supine sex ad,
swathed in a glitz of blinking bulbs,
for you to come and unwrap.

Like Esméralda, but Luckier

Like Esméralda I sit,
dark haired and white skinned,
on a versicoloured bed,
a red mohair blanket at my feet,
golden cushions at my back.

She mock-suckles her goat,
and I, an invisible baby.
Unlike Esméralda, however,
I did not choose love
with the wrong man.

To Gretna Green

after Chagall

Nobody will help us
on our bridal run:
not my sisters,
not his ganger from
the tartan mill.

We creep through
the empty village
where my parents sleep,
a low-slung moon
lights our way.

I take my broad-backed
hen with me for eggs,
for the company;
a shock of heather
as my bouquet.

He grips me tight on the
march to Gretna Green,
and all I can think is
Why, oh, why
must we run away?

Portrait of the Artist with a Red Car

Three Polish boys battle with their car on the garage forecourt; up they push it, down they swing it, but the car won't loosen up. It all looks as tough as waltzing with an anchor. I watch their dance through my murky windscreen, sodden in the smells of discarded food, of damp; safe with an engine that always thrums to life, eventually. And I wish for better cars for all of us: for them, a Volvo estate, swift and reliable; for myself, a cherry-red Mini that will zip and glide, park in less than five arm-pulling points. Then I remember my last red car, and wonder if too much pride in its spanky redness left it a rusted heap in a Donegal scrap-yard; whether crashing it started the slow wreckage of our marriage.

Guilt

Guilt is never to be doubted
— KAFKA

Stuck like an oyster in my throat,
it is a choking, meaty valve
that sputters saltwater and
threatens slowly to drown me.

I will cough it up,
dislodge its fat rubber grip
and swallow easily again,
only if I can forgive myself.

Mistress

I am   the music of the one who is tricked
       the song that should never be sung

I am   the mother of no memory
       the daughter of discomfort

I am   the shout that breaks outwards
       the laughter that seldom sounds

I am   the night that cannot converse with itself
       the day that is misplaced or stolen

I am   the bright morning that grows wet
       the evening that has to end somewhere

I am   the water that smells of weed and stone
       the fire of coal then ash, of ash then coal

I am   the change that bullets over the horizon
       the heart folded back, not as it was

I am   the breaking straw in their union
       the loved only because I am leaving.

Anger

The moon is battered tonight, bruised and swollen,
but she swanks above us, bringing joy to the chill.

Tallow moon, electric moon, she shoulders the sky,
a brazen spotlight over trees salted with frost.

Down here, eyes aching, we creep to the church
on the square and make peace with each other in song.

Clouds

after Basho

The clouds part from time to time
and bring us the chance to rest,
to marvel at the moon.

Monthly

Tonight the moon is Plathic,
she is not my mother,
but her O-face cries out like
a hole punched in the sky.

She pulls on me like sea-suck
and pushes clouds down to earth
to smother my peace, crush me –
this is her monthly curse.

I curse her too, this pearl dropped in ink:
knuckle moon, skull moon,
you will soon wane, but my mind
will settle back into my body.

Menses

Before the butterfly days
are the fly days,
and before those,
the days of the spiders,
and along with them
come the waiting days.
The mind asks the body
if it is happening,
invisible and unseen,
a cell-dividing miracle.
The answer comes
on too many of these
long summer days,
drop by red drop.

The Juno Charm

for Finbar

I am the pomegranate
and you, the peacock

My seedy, red-pulped core
glistens with juice,
awaits your entrance

Your erectile feathers
flash ocellated spots,
they wink with promise

Amulet

I wear a hummingbird at my throat
its wing-beats trapped in silver,
I hear it clear across continents and seas
a hopeful sound from another world.

In Galway, magpies fly in ones and ones,
I salute each bird, scan the sky for pairs.

Maybe, in Tierra del Fuego,
a woman wears a silver magpie
at her throat, hoping it will bring
an end to ill luck, to sorrow.

An Unlucky Woman

I will pluck charms, dangle them
from my neck and the headboard:
rose-quartz beads and a silver turtle,
a Síle-na-Gig with gaping lips.

I will visit the rag tree at Clonfert,
pin a baby's soother to its trunk,
carry a discreet pouch of hazelnuts,
slip two gilded fish under our bed.

I will wear a Saint Gerard scapular,
the kind of thing that drips miracles,
and just maybe this army of amulets
will make my body do what it won't.

There Are Seeds in My Soup

I store them in my teeth
like amulets, tucked away
for a later reunion with
my tongue, my throat, my belly.

They are the heart trinkets
of a November squash
that I hacked into fleshy cubes
to make my soup butter-soft.

These seeds talk of earthy things
– soil, vines, snuffling badgers –
they whisper hope from my mouth:
'We will fatten you, fill you out.'

I winnow them from my teeth,
swallow each one whole and
wait for them to do their work,
the seeds I have found in my soup.

August in Monaghan

Lumbering cattle kick loose
on both sides of my car

Montbretia blazes and nods
from every hedgerow

Drumlins hump and skitter
as far away as I can see

A meandering one-eared dog
ignores my warning toot

The Black Kesh crumbles,
all its revellers long gone

A papery frog crouches,
nonchalant, under my door

Blue dragonflies shimmy
over Annaghmakerrig lake

And my baby grows in the quiet:
stealthy, secret, sweet.

Foetal

we are fastened to our bed
you curl to the curl of me
unshaped to a shape that fits

we sleep, curved into one
and my body begins
the slow, good work

work that weakens me,
balloons me with
both hope and dread

then, after three months,
the heartsick, two-letter slip,
from foetal to fatal

Miscarriage and Dream

When I looked at the snow-field screen
where you were helplessly *sous neige*,
I knew I would see only a static curl.
My heart slowed to breaking, to match yours,
stopped.

That night, the Virgin statue came to life
and took your unformed body in her hands,
she popped you in her mouth and smiled.

Sons

We are knitted
unpickably to each other,
a weave of bone and blood,
words spoken and unsaid,
an unassailable love,
at least from my side.

But if, in years to come,
you both unstitch
yourselves from me,
I will try not to let the
yarn snag, but ravel free,
an unwinding of need.

A Sort of Couvade

There is a distance in me, a removal
from this, my last pregnancy,
few chinks let in the possibility
of a positive *coup de grâce*
to end all the years of strife and faith.

I dream other people's babies,
ones who refuse to suckle,
so I hand them back to be
cauled in their mother's love,
but still my baby labours in me,
adding lanugo and vernix
to her cornucopia of miracles,
positing layers of fat
that will insulate her
when she delivers herself to us
in the cool-aired birthing suite,
borne down by my body's rhythms,
because and in spite of me.

Wrapped in a battledress of
grease, blood and bruising,
she will wear me like a crown
before forcing through, pulling labia taut,
and I will be present because
that is what I am made for,
I will perform a sort of *couvade*
at my only daughter's birth.

Die Schwangere

~ pregnant in Karlsruhe ~

The other poets drink damson schnapps
from thistle-head glasses,

My baby flicker-kicks
with all five ounces of her weight,
with all four inches of her length.

I dream her hand
pipping from the egg of my belly
like a wing through shell,
I hold her embryonic fingers,
thrilling at her light touch.

Delighting in my blooming belly,
I feel my nestled passenger,
she flicks and settles, settles and kicks;
her cells gather, graceful as an origami swan
in perfect folds and re-folds.

In perfect folds and re-folds
her cells gather, graceful as an origami swan
she flicks and settles, settles and kicks;
I feel my nestled passenger
delighting in my blooming belly.

Thrilling at her light touch
I hold her embryonic fingers,
like a wing through shell,
pipping from the egg of my belly,
I dream her hand.

With all four inches of her length,
with all five ounces of her weight,
my baby flicker-kicks.

From thistle-head glasses
the other poets drink damson schnapps.

Nightfeed

I elbow-cradle her plump;
she grunts and guzzles,
unsuckles, then surveys me
with one squint eye.

A pearl of milk slips
from nipple to lips
into the oyster of her ear;
she smiles, re-nuzzles.

Peabiddy

for Juno at 18 months

The flaps opened and out you popped,
biddy-in-the-box, one wing raised
in a super-heroine's salute.

We put you there, cock and hen,
rattling feathers and shrieking softly
under canvas in a midland field.

You, our emerald peabiddy,
the actual fact of you musters pride
as we watch amazed at your evolution.

How you stomp on sturdy legs and
perfect your calls: the eee-ow of your tribe,
the vowels and consonants of ours.

Safe passage – we cannot fly with you –
but our nest will always be here and
we can guarantee a soft landing.

The Japanese Madonna

As Madonna of Akita
I was carved
by a Buddhist from
a weeping katsura.

I forsook kimono and zori
for an unpainted robe,
a European chin,
and an aristocrat's gaze.

I dropped blood-tears,
my sweat stank of roses,
and I warned that fire
would fall from the sky.

In Ballinspittle
I was made of stone;
I just flexed my fingers
and rocked.

Death, Water and Woman

L'Inconnue was not
plucked from the river
by la Brigade Fluviale,
like a freshwater trout.

She was not propped
on a slab in the morgue's
window to be peered at
by hungry Parisians.

She did not pick woman's
preferred mode of suicide –
a languid drowning;
men, they say, prefer the rope.

No, her Junoesque vigour
and serene smile give her away:
she was quite well when
her death-mask was shaped.

Galway

While Galway swells both
sides of the stony Corrib,
her macaronic voice echoes
with car horn, horse hoof and
the tok-tok of harbour boats,
drunk with Spanish sailors.

All the air is fish-reeky where
Nimmo's Pier points a long
lazy arm to Black Head,
and the suck of the sea
pulls the eye to Salthill,
soaked under April storms.

Skirling origami swans decorate
the Claddagh basin while Galway
settles her night-shawl down,
boats and birds safe at her breast.
And her poets – all of her poets –
are upfront about love.

Belle Bilton of Ballinasloe

In 1889, Isabel Bilton, an English music hall singer, married Viscount Dunlo; she became Lady Dunlo and, later, Countess of Clancarty in Ballinasloe, County Galway.

Viscount Dunlo won much in that coin-toss for my hand.
The Goddess Venus is not just a part that I play;
My beauty saw my man cut off from his land.

They said I was a wanton and my Viscount half-mad,
His father tried to cleave us, sent my husband away.
Viscount Dunlo won much in that coin-toss for my hand.

My love sailed to Australia with my heart in his hands
I took comfort with another, by night and by day,
My beauty saw my man cut off from his land.

The life that I craved played out only in dreamlands.
My husband might not return from Botany Bay.
Viscount Dunlo won much in that coin-toss for my hand.

His father pressed our divorce, the way the wealthy can.
I sang for my life, for what was I permitted to say?
My beauty saw my man cut off from his land.

My Viscount came back, vowed not to leave again.
We had four sons and a daughter, our love led the way.
Viscount Dunlo won much in that coin-toss for my hand.
My beauty saw my man returned to his land.

Weather, East Galway

I

A whale-cloud swims over Ballinasloe,
baleen hanging in chalky strips –
it drips fat drops from Brackernagh to Beagh.

II

Mallards arse-dive in the tea-coloured Suck
like teenage boys let loose in summer
while fog eats up the trees on the bank.

III

Hubcap leaves scuttle along Society Street,
the Virgin Mary gentles over Bully's Acre,
petals with plastic raindrops at her feet.

IV

A swan-family jets over a snowy M6,
they are white arrows against zinc,
one is the seventh cygnet of a seventh swan.

Inland Resort

The Derwent gorges underneath
the Jubilee Bridge, seeking wide water.

In Linda's Plaice there are lovebirds for sale;
I wonder aloud what saveloys are
while relishing their Olivertwistian sound.

Outside the river calls – as all rivers call –
missing its mouth, surely, the swim-rings
and spades, shrimp nets and sail boats,
the wide bucket of the sea.

Destination

it is a slice of Tokyo, cut and pasted into the skyline,
a salmon, leapt up from the Liffey, scales gleaming,
a Narcissus, admiring his reflection in the river water,
a theatre of labour, crystal curtain dropped to the stage,
a tea caddy, cauled by a pagoda of green water-wave.

Landmark

On the Eden of the quays
she is the loftiest tree,
the first skyscraper,
a maverick.
She holds the city below
in a shimmering embrace,
marking the land, at liberty.

Over Water

In the Liffey murk,
a water-glass reflection
that floats over
a stray seal,
shopping trolleys,
a corpse,
eels.

Gull

On the rooftop of this urban aurora,
a gull, strayed up from a squat Martello,
shapes her eyes to the view:

a ballet of cranes, vying for space,
swinging down on the skyline of the bay,

green trains darting to Howth, Bray,
and less lofty points between;

the bridges that bracelet the river,
each named for a different man;

copper domes and yellow buses;
the slender finger of the Spire.

She beaks the air, lets fly.

Nineteen-Seventy-Two

a layer of glass, a layer of concrete,
a layer of concrete, a layer of glass,
a gossamer chamber of light became
a hall of mirrors, after the bomb blast.

··· — — — ···

The sun sparks off windows
each pane a glass semaphore
knocking a message out to bungalows
hunkered in the Dublin Mountains,
an SOS that says: *I am near my end.*

And the bungalows wink back:
Weren't towers made to be razed?

Cherry Blossom Haiku

weeping sakura –
your blossom tears puddle to
a pink petal quilt

Mute

You smile, Leda, suspecting this is not a swan,
but man as swan: he purrs and wheedles;
a real mute, you know, would launch a direct attack.

Cradling his neck, you let his taut breast push
against your leg and he too seems to smile,
his upper mandible lifting in pleasure.

His feathers – they would delight any *plumassier* –
tickle your skin and each wing-flick sends
a rush of blood to the valley of your thighs.

But when he rears up on black feet, wingspan huge,
understains on his plumage alarm you,
the dirt there speaks of river-mud and secrets.

He pins you down, enters you with a ragged pain.
You scream inside and a stray thought flies:
When he dies, will he sing?

Kingfisher Sister

In the halcyon hours of winter solstice,
you loosened your grip
for the slip towards death.

You had no mate to hoist you on his back
and fly over the flat-calm sea,
mourning you with his cries.

But in your last storm, *a thaisce*, never fear,
our sorrow saw you safely
into the blue, in a blaze of red.

Mannequin Envy

It's not the pert plum breasts
or the bloodless complexion

It's not the gamine gait
or the fuck-me-please eyes

It's the luxurious laziness
of her shop-window leisure,

the loitering with no intent.

Frida Kahlo Visits Ballinasloe

Frida Kahlo likes to walk in colour,
but she is hard pushed on Society Street.

We wander together up Sarsfield Road;
'Where is all the yellow,' she asks, 'the red?'

Frida, in a floral dress and Mexican silver,
draws a tidings of magpies from the sky.

'No parrots,' she says, 'no hibiscus?'
Clouds part, a triangle of blue pleases her.

Then she sees a scarlet Massey Ferguson,
yew berries spilled like beads on the footpath,

A woman in a crimson coat and man's shoes,
a King Charles with a postcard colleen's curls,

Tail-lights like alien eyes spinning to Ahascragh;
'Viva la vida,' says unflinching Frida, painter of pain.

She sings the reds of Sarsfield Road and they bleed
into the veins of the town, pulsing its grey.

A Cézanne Nude

I stand as still
as a fruit on a plate.

My breasts are plums,
my behind a peach.

Monsieur says if I move,
he will pulp me.

So I hand him
my daguerreotype

and leave the door open
on my way out.

Yellow

In the asylum, I am secure from it.
These grey walls hold nothing of sunshine,
spring flowers, butter or lemons.

Here I miss my *Woman Rocking a Cradle*:
her pillowed chest and beatific gaze,
the dahlias that sing from the wallpaper.

But I must also remember, she is the
unruly Madonna, the gold-faced mocker
who made me cut a slitch off my ear.

The flesh-slice I parcelled in newspaper
and gifted to my favourite streetwalker,
who smiled, unwrapped, and fainted at the sight.

All in the name of yellow.

Sien

*'In Antwerp Van Gogh fell in love with a prostitute who
consented to be his model, a pock-marked, pregnant tramp
in the last stages of drunkenness.'*

        – THOMAS CRAVEN

Sien, see how history files us:
you, pocked, pissed and pregnant,
me, the lunatic painter, taken in.

Nothing is said of our dimensions:
the beauty of your baby-heavy body,
or your hair, tailing down your back.

And what of my electric joy when
your newborn son lit up the hospital bed,
a bright Messiah dropped among us?

No, posterity will not sympathise with us,
or add loving blood to pump our hearts.
But I – of course – get off lighter than you.

Domestic Slave, Sweeping Up

after Joyce Little's artwork

Me and myself,
we are a harlequin pair:
me, neat-shaven,
myself, lavish with hair.

I try to decide
which me I prefer:
me, neat-shaven,
myself, sprackled with hair.

Neat-shaven, I don't moult,
leave strands everywhere;
hirsute, I sweep all day
to keep the house free of hair.

Yes, me and myself,
we are a harlequin pair:
me, neat-shaven,
myself, a slave to my hair.

Woman and Cosmetics

after Wayne Thiebaud's painting

My mother's legacy of white skin,
my father's of fertile girth:
this is my canvas.

All my life I have tried to alter
what was decreed in the womb.

With five shades of lipstick:
Ice Pink, Rosé Requinqué, Macao,
Café Latté, Lady Bug.

With fake-flesh concealer and
pots of eyeshadow, bruise-blue.

I brush and rub, pencil and shade –
trying to make a more palatable
woman of the woman that I am.

La Reine

The smells are all drain and hot scalp;
my stylist installs me in front of a mirror,
combs in silence with lunatic ferocity.
For others her mouth is as big as Galway Bay;
we, it seems, don't share a language.

My hair falls to the floor in wet apostrophes,
the stylist pushes me under the hood;
part crown, part throne, it is called La Reine.
I sit, Marie Antoinette, head burning;
my plan, however, is to get out alive.

The End of Constance

I saw her polonaise before I saw her,
a turquoise frippery tucked all over –
a milkmaid's gown gone mad;
Mother heard she had come from London.

London is not Myshall, it is shadowed
by glass and brick; here the grassy flanks
of Mount Leinster loom over the plain;
I wondered how long she would last.

Last summer Inglis Brady wooed me,
we rode the heather slopes together
fashioning our future with glances,
out of words we built an understanding.

Understanding that he would stray
if I left him to follow his heart,
I slipped a bur under her saddle.
At the Nine Stones the mare threw her.

Her parents erected a memorial,
they called it 'a statue of innocence.'
Six months after the accident,
Inglis Brady took my hand.

Two Children Are Threatened
by a Nightingale

after Max Ernst

Max Ernst saw an eye, a nose, a bird's head,
a menacing nightingale and a spinning top
in an innocent knot of wood by his bed.

I see faces in the Rorschach pattern
of the curtains, a profile of a man,
snoot-nosed and Victorian, condemning us.

I dream I am in South Africa with a former lover.
We dodge bullets and buy postcards
of old houses; we touch each other's skin.

My son, worried by lightning, pulls out
the plugs all over the house; he stands still
at the window, wondering if airplanes will fall.

And I don't dare to tell him that airplanes do fall,
that people condemn, and that there is menace in more
than paintings of children threatened by a nightingale.

Sofa

I squat by a farm-gate like a sneaky pisser,
hunched low, arms bent, wearing ruin heavily.

Domestic glories are gone: no more coin caches,
scattered plumpy cushions, or copulating couples.

My lap is torn velour that belches foam and springs
around arse-shaped dinges and unnameable stains.

But despite being careworn, I am still useful:
my insides are a womb to a mischief of mice.

Thai Maid

The sheet bloats and gullies over her head,
the white sail of my surrender to this
block-on-ugly-block hotel in Münich.

She instructs me on necessary shortcuts:
the fast flick of hot water on a sink,
how to pick at lint instead of Hoovering.

As tiny as a wren, she toils and chatters,
pushing me on with ten times my strength,
one hundred times my good humour.

Poem Beginning with a Line by Plath

This is the light of the mind, cold and planetary,
it keeps me solitary, stumbling inside paranoia.

My anchoritic needs are not a bow to religion,
they are as prosaic as any modern-day hermit's:

who is there to trust with the black of my heart, when
some trample, some steal what's mine for their own?

For Olive, the Unknown

For the child I was,
the one who said
That's a horrible name,
all I can say is *Sorry.*
Your name holds centuries.
It is the glossy drupe
snug around the pit,
as meaty as a kalamata.

But it was unripe
– a slippy green ascalano –
to my young girl's ears.
So with oil of the sun, Olive,
with cold oil, virgin oil,
and grass-smelling oil,
I beg now to gift you
the beauty of your name.

The Hen Whisperer

The hen sits on the dry-stone wall,
my palms collaring her neck;
we face each other, lip to beak,
her comb and wattle jiddering.

Fingering her feathers, I cluck,
forming a burble of hen-speak:
'Remember pipping through the violet
membrane; think of your egg-tooth.'
My hands gather around her plump,
mimicking a shell, her safest place.

But this hen is having none of it;
she swells her feathers and pecks,
flusters from the wall and struts off;
she is this coop's renegade chicken,
an untameable maverick, a ne'er do well.

The Cat and the Man

Today a white cat, clean as new paper, cut across my path;
in the post office, a man wore tattoos as easy as clothing:

wings on his nape, the better to fly,
green clover under his ear, for good fortune,

a quaver on his neck, to keep him singing,
and the name Gretchen, to remind him to love.

His buzz-cut and checkerboard runners were pedestrian,
but his skin glowed in that queue of farmers and housewives;
he was his own canvas, a heart's sleeve of obsessions.

I wanted to unbutton his shirt to see what was inked
on the throat of his wrist, his chest, his back;
to read the whole of his story.

On Being Irish

Caged birds watch starlings swoop.
'Bloody show-offs,' they tweet.
Begrudgerigars.

Flirt

He speaks butcherese to me,
all rump and breast and heart
while his fingers fumble
among drisheen and tongue,
searching for a choice cut,
or a little sweetmeat to tempt me.

He sways in a blood-stiff apron,
tips his mesh trilby coyly;
I gaze at a pink china pig
that stands frozen among
crubeens and puce livers,
a grove of plastic parsley.

I refuse to mince words,
'A bag of breadcrumbs, please.'
On my way out, I toe graffiti
into the sawdust: *I heart tofu*,
then flick a glance his way.
He cuts me with his eyes.

Dancing with Paul Durcan

I saw Paul Durcan in The Winding Stair,
fingering a book of love sonnets.
'Paul,' I said, 'your poetry is filthy with longing.'
He said, 'Would you like to dance?'

So breast to chest we turned a Durcanesque
polka of long poems and harem-scarem
happenings around the bookstacks.

And, oh, the heft of him.

'I won't be falling in love with you,' I said,
'That's OK,' Paul murmured, 'love's not
looking for me at the moment. We've fallen out.'

Our bodies collided into man-woman as we swung,
our clothes and skin sewn into each other,
our legs a kicking chorus of dance, dance, dance.

Paul spun me down the winding stairs,
up across the bow of the Ha'penny Bridge,
and, spinning together, all our pages flew.

Puberty

after Andrew Wyeth's painting

There is no jouncing for the girl
in the pink shirt-waister:
she is prone, like any painted female,
she is feline, and her face is not painted.

Her Thinking Place is a field
widening to a horizon that holds
a barn, a house and two sheds,
erect as gravestones on the skyline.

She would crawl there if she could,
enter the house, like womanhood,
but for now she waits, a cat in the grass,
stalking what lies ahead.

Lumière Noir

I

Sunday in Kilchreest, a car
drives into the graveyard, stops.

The driver stands, head cocked,
questioning a headstone.

Her car door is swung wide,
ready for the getaway.

Cows cluster on hills, daffodils
ruffling their ankles, waiting.

II

The beads on the lampshade
make a skull of the light bulb.

It gapes down at me in my bath,
a put-together *memento mori*.

My mind lives under a gaslight
hardly letting in mortality's possibility.

But tonight, under this *lumière noir*,
I accept death – the other side.

Insomnia

Not one of my soporific tricks work
but I haul them out each night:

one, Mississippi
two, Mississippi
three, Mississippi
four.

White sheets, white clouds, paper,
unwritten-on pages rolling to a blank horizon,

but the plain, unpainted sheets soon turn to snow,
then clouds; to contrails, aeroplanes and holidays.

I don't count sheep;
they're too substantial
with their maiden-aunt faces,
chawing on grass like so many facts,
fixing me with one all-knowing eye,
their unbearably beautiful lambs
suckling in the netherlands of their
curled woollen coats.

Not one of my soporific tricks work
so I have to begin again:

white sheets, white clouds, paper,
unwritten-on pages rolling to a blank horizon.

One, Mississippi
two, Mississippi
three, Mississippi
four.

Blue House, Magdalen Islands, Quebec

Here's me, a loner,
like the namesake
of the islands
where I perch

under a violet sky,
above a sea
that turns to ice,
an unsafe winter road.

On the horizon
sister islands hump
low like whales:
La Grosse Île, Île d'Entrée.

Another house calls
to me across the sound,
it speaks in a voice
only we can understand.

Adam and Eve as Entrepreneurs

After Eden, and all that palaver with Yahweh,
dust and flesh, fruit and asp, fig leaves and so forth,
we were in the market for a new place.

I fancied somewhere lofty: a tree-house with a view.
But my chap had had it with trees, and wanted
something darkly comforting, like a cave.

We hustled the deposit for an artisan's dwelling,
converted the downstairs, and swung a sign outside:
'Adam & Eve, Purveyors of Human Kind, since Time Began'.

Himself manned the office, paring pencils,
waiting for business to boom. I languished in our bed,
belly ripening, waiting for the daughter I was sure would come.

The Writer's Room

after The Guardian's photographs

My desk was a present from Margaret Atwood.
After *Zen and the Art of Uterus Maintenance*
sold its first million, she said I needed a place
to write, other than the local bus-shelter.

My view is of the bare wall, of course;
the window and the street are too distracting
for a mind as relentlessly creative as mine –
the very leaves on the trees inspire me.

I picked up the rug on a trek in Uzbekistan,
and that basque-shaped card is from Madonna –
she just adored my last little offering:
The Sex of a Good Enough Woman.

My chair, as you can see, is a bale of hay.
I will always be a simple farmer's daughter,
with that need to stay close to natural things;
my oak shelves were salvaged from the Titanic.

My computer is Sony's latest – *trés* posh –
but I, of course, prefer paper and ink, then
I bash out a final draft on my Remington,
and let my super editor deal with it all.

Have you bought the new collection yet,
Back-pedalling from Hell on My Menstrual Cycle?
It's sort of Paul Muldoon meets Wendy Cope,
with a dash of Famous Séamus, for gravitas.

My agent says it will be my biggest book to date,
so I've left space on the shelf for a few gongs:
The T.S. Eliot, the *Irish Times*, the Nobel –
I'll be content with whatever comes my way.

Yes, it's in this humble room – where I am
unassailable – that all the magic begins.

Nuala Ní Chonchúir is a novelist, poet and short fiction writer. She was born in Dublin in 1970 and educated at Trinity College, Dublin, Dublin City University and NUI Galway. Her first full poetry collection *Molly's Daughter* appeared in the ¡DIVAS! Anthology *New Irish Women's Writing* (Arlen House). Her bilingual poetry collection *Tattoo:Tatú* (Arlen House, 2007) was shortlisted for the 2008 Rupert and Eithne Strong Award. A pamphlet *Portrait of the Artist with a Red Car* (Templar, 2009) was one of four winners of the 2009 Templar Poetry Pamphlet competition.

Nuala's début novel *You* (New Island, 2010) was called 'a heart-warmer' by *The Irish Times* and 'a gem' by *The Irish Examiner*. Her third short story collection *Nude* (Salt, 2009) was shortlisted for the Edge Hill Prize.

Nuala teaches creative writing part-time and has won many literary prizes, including RTÉ Radio's Francis MacManus Award, the inaugural Cúirt New Writing Prize, the inaugural Jonathan Swift Award and the Cecil Day Lewis Award. She has twice been nominated for a Hennessy Award, and was awarded Arts Council Bursaries in Literature in 2004 and 2009.

Her poetry and fiction have been published and anthologised in Ireland, the UK, France, Canada, Australia and the USA; and have been broadcast on RTÉ Radio 1 and Lyric FM. Her residencies have included a poetry writing project with long-term elderly residents in Merlin Park Hospital, Galway, and Writer-in-Residence at the Cúirt International Festival of Literature. Nuala lives in County Galway with her husband and three children.

www.nualanichonchuir.com